Selected moments of machine life

A collection of poems and paintings

AF328462

Pete Ramskill is a poet, artist, designer and sculptor.
He used to perform regularly on Terry Christian's Radio Derby show
and has performed at the Edinburgh Festival for BBC Radio 4.
He also appeared on BBC 3's *Whine Gums* poetry series.
Pete has performed at poetry and cabaret venues all over the UK.

Other poetry by Pete Ramskill

Some of the poems in this collection
previously appeared in:
Strike (Derby Co-operative Press 1985)
Personal Vendetta (The Amazing Colossal Press 1989)

Pete's paintings have been exhibited at:
Terre Verte Gallery, Altarnun, Cornwall
Ruddington Manor
Mish Mash Gallery, Chilwell, Nottingham

Front cover painting:
Waiting in Winter
Acrylics and inks on paper 57 x 76cm

Selected moments of machine life
A collection of poems and paintings

Pete Ramskill

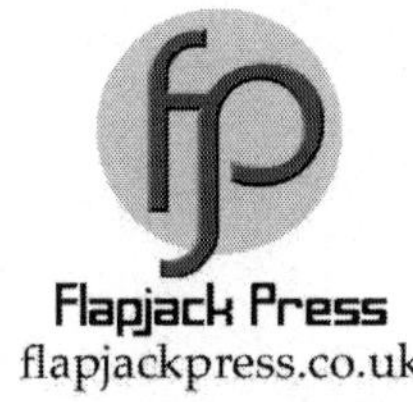

Flapjack Press
flapjackpress.co.uk
Exploring the synergy between performance and the page

Published in 2018 by Flapjack Press
Salford, Gtr Manchester
flapjackpress.co.uk

ISBN 978-0-9955012-8-7

All rights reserved
Copyright © Pete Ramskill, 2018

peteramskilldesign.co.uk

Back cover photo by Orson Ramskill Pugh

Printed by Imprint Digital
Upton Pyne, Exeter, Devon
imprintdigital.com

This book is sold subject to the condition that is shall not by way of
trade or otherwise be lent, re-sold, hired out or otherwise circulated
in any form, binding or cover other than that in which it is published
and without a similar condition including this condition being imposed
on the subsequent purchaser.

Dedicated to Reggie, Orson, Alfie
and my sister Sarah

And with thanks to Henry Normal
for his friendship and nagging support

Contents

Foreword

The thing I love most about all Pete's work, and the very essence
of the man, is that he is decisive.

There's something solid and true about his approach. He has
the courage of his convictions. Not that he doesn't display
vulnerability or sensitivity in his poetry and art. I believe he excels
in that, but at the core there appears something that will not bend
and refuses to break.

Over the past twenty years I've seen his poetry, his sculptures,
his design work and his paintings, and they are all unmistakably
his own. I love his sense of self-expression and seeing him discover
and pursue his originality with such passion that I find
it inspirational.

There are many other things I love about this work. Pete's Stanley-
knife sense of humour, his intelligence, invention, precision,
quality control and his radar for those lies, injustices and petty
sins that he cannot bring himself to see swept under the carpet.
I love his use of language, his original images, his exposure of
those everyday social earthquakes and especially those bits people
think they've got past him but he reveals they haven't.

I am very proud to be asked to write this foreword and hope you
enjoy Pete's work as much as I do. To see him read these poems
live will add emphasis on all these qualities, as will seeing the
paintings in real life.

This book captures some of the powerful life-force he brings
to his creativity. Don't just tiptoe in. Be decisive. Commit.

Henry Normal

I once misread a sign in an Oxfam shop
'We will not live with poverty' I read as
We will not live with poetry

Poetry leaves a solemn stink
Its whisky breath and other drink
Poetry is a waste of ink
A pallid world of pale pink

Reams and reams and yet more reams
Of clever couplets in rhyming schemes
Living in diaphanous dreams
Don't even know what that means

Alive with limp alliteration
Lapping tonguing masturbation
Sycophantic sonnets for the nation
An allegoric aberration

The meter running to the measure
The stanzas scanning at your leisure
The laureate's a national treasure
A pulsing pentameter of pleasure

But then when it can get no worse
The utterly depraved perverse
Blank verse
Which is nothing more
Than never ending
Sentences
Broken up randomly
With line breaks
But very little punctuation
And sometimes
Not even a capital letter
In sight
Just nonstop
Words going on and on
Under the moonlight
Till the whole thing stops
Suddenly

The shits - badly

on Saturdays
I used to go to
the cafe where the pretty-young-things
would hang out
and I'd draw them filling
their faces
and all the time I was really
trying to impress the girl
who only just managed a smile as
she served out
piss-poor coffee

maybe she knew how bad it was

eleven years later I'm here again
and there's another girl
and she's even more beautiful

I feel old
I don't live in this town any more
I know enough now to impress this new girl
but I don't try

she serves me a sandwich
which gives me the shits for two days

it beats dieting and exercise

I'm trying not to look down
But I'm six floors up
Carrying a few pounds and an iced drink
By a rooftop pool

The price of my flight
Would keep you for a year or more
The price of this iced drink
Would feed all of you for a day

I'm trying not to look down
As you shuffle about
Laughing and nonstop natter
Busy as bees
And pissing in the bushes

You tidy your mattresses
All you possess
Whilst downstairs
My sons' room
Is like an explosion in a clothing factory

I'm trying not to look down
On all this perfect dignity
On values that we have hidden
I'm trying not to look down
At smiles that say you are the ones
who have everything

I'm trying not to look down
When I should be looking up

Florescent fruit and rotten veg

You walk in... look around... look about... check it out
shopping in the supermarket
sunglasses in the pocket
ready for the situation... for the confrontation
with the whitest of white cabbage
the brightest of cauliflowers
so white it's like a bloody strobe-light
blinding, frightening
finding, lined up
lime green lettuces
better get a Geiger-counter
want to know why they glow

fruit in florescent shades
apples in the A-grade
giving off gamma-rays
bright red, overfed
on Baby-Bio
Smooth as billiard balls
BLACK berries, BLACK currants, BLACK cherries

beetroots in jack-boots
regimented demented damsons
despot potatoes
with no eyes
don't know what to buy
onions to make you cry
genocide for greenfly
LET THE IMPERFECTS DIE

The mangos are man-made
peaches are on parade
RED peppers perfect skin
but WHO let the parsnips in ?

Bananas in day-glo
totalitarian tomatoes
arian avocados
chemical coleslaw
introduced martial law

radish rotten in the store
radioactive to the core

cucumbers... in numbers
neo-nazi... nationalistic
never had a nectarine or green grape
from the Cape
can't take fresh fruits
that have their roots
in straight arm salutes

Conversation

How are you?

GOOD
you said
and it sounded true
inarguable
and not at all open to question

the complete answer

GOOD

slightly abrupt
not exactly multi-faceted
not exactly detailed
and I'm sure it can't apply to every aspect
to every part
to every... whatever!

GOOD

the thing is
what do you say next?

GOOD

the first and the last
a conversation up and running
over and done
a single swing of the sword
across the throat
Bang!

GOOD

a four letter word
that denies access
closes doors
moves the point of reference
changes nothing
confirms everything
expresses a certainty with clarity
and raises a dim candle
to a cultural diversity

GOOD

seems like this is the time to decide
whether this is unbridgeable
or
great entertainment
and a time for investigation

GOOD

it may be colloquial
but
put that way
it sounds like a good time for exploration

Telephone

I'm developing an obsession with the telephone
it sits there
like something savoury in the fridge
after a few beers

irresistible

but, no matter what happened
no matter how much
or how little
I loved each one of you
you're all somewhere else now
in love
a little
or a lot
with someone new

and so the phone just sits there
and I dip into the fridge
for another beer
and a slice of salami

Over the road
a woman of strange proportions
two hinged squares
languid lumbering after the dog
with her watering can
like some crazed shepherd-rain-goddess
rounding up the dripping mutt

And the neighbours
looked askance in amusement
and told me
how bastard rattlers
would find it tough round here
and end up skinned
and hung from lines
by them bastard kids
who piss in your milk bottles...

Dots

I have a magazine
in which there is a series of photographs

They show a man
bearded
about thirty years old
with one arm tied to a tree
The other arm
is tied to a jeep

In a few frames
the jeep moves left to right

Strange

One arm tears away
The arm tied to the tree
For some reason
I expected it to be the other arm

The man's face is stretched into a scream
that looks like it would be too high pitched to hear
And I wondered if
just for a moment
before the pain
the absurd question entered his thoughts
about which arm would tear

And I wondered about the black dots
on the paper
making up the pictures

Pictures that hide the smells
and keep us deaf
and keep us sat on our flabby arses...

In Prague
          the Pan Am poster read
'Take the world by the tail'
and I was twelve

I was twelve
          when the cobblestones clattered
under metal tracks
cat scratch blood lines through Kafka's dreams
and there they stood
the young heroes of anti-revisionism
Bemused boys
with mother's farewell kiss
          still wet on stubble free faces
The faces of tomorrow
Questions jabbing
          sunburning into their eyes
as the pleas of innocence evaporated in the air
with the spring mist's revelations
They smiled to stop the tears of incomprehension
          and posed for photos
One man's heroes
          another man's lowest level lackeys
fit only for vilification and spit

Unnoticed, through the city
through all the cities
the imperturbable rivers strolled and winked
like wise old men and women telling tales

Elsewhere, the masked banditos
built their barricades
not far from chauffeur driven cars
and hurled their frustrations
with protruding flames like tiny wings
carrying the ideals of an age
to shatter into life on concrete
The last rights of the last mad-cap flickering dance
Till next time
Bugs-of-the-night

Caught

Caught in the dream-boat conveyor belt
Lost in the kaleidoscopic superstore
Caught in the dark day of a nightshift
Lost to the silent scream of a horoscope

He never wanted to hit anyone
till he saw her cry over a soap opera
sucked up by the insincerity
and still he didn't want to hit HER
just someone

He rubbed his eyes
as if this would reveal the next scene

He didn't see the love
in the laugh
that crushed him
like moths' wings
fluttering in his face

In a quiet moment of uncertainty
a voice said
'know yourself'
and was followed by silence

Then, another voice
less familiar
assured yet unconcerned said
'all that is not known
is in doubt'
causing a reflection and a chill

Closed eyes confirmed the darkness
and in the shadows of darkness
a third voice
rose slowly
and sang a soothing song
in sensual tones affirming
'there is only doubt'

STRIKE I - the unlikely battlefields

Through time's forgotten places
Restored by middle-class opulence
Past the languid farms and fields
of the safe and sleeping Midlands
Until ahead
emerges
The careless scattered communities
of England's industrial outposts
Hidden in the dips and hollows
in a fairy-ring of rust brown skeletons
of previous generations
with the dull clanging of dead doors
and broken window eyes watching
over the grey lines of houses
Strangely silent
Almost apologising
for disturbing rural scenes
Innocent in isolation

The 'STRIKE' poems are based on conversations with miners
from South Wales, Derbyshire and South Yorkshire during
the miners' strike of 1984 -85.

STRIKE II - in defence of a way of life
(during the miners' strike most miners picketed
their own pits or pits in their area)

"There are police from everywhere
  Places only heard of in the news
  or places never heard of at all
  Places seen on maps and road signs
  Unknown towns and cities
  with accents only heard on TV
  or in radio plays
  Occasional words without meaning
  And they are here
  in places that THEY do not know
  or understand
  They are here
  in OUR homes
  OUR towns and villages
  They are here
  denying us dignity
  in OUR places
  Road-blocks in OUR streets
  Stopped on OUR doorsteps
  Abused in our own homes
  in the places where we live now
  in the places where we must live
  when they have gone"

STRIKE III - father and son

You sit warm
with coffee-cupped hand
with slippered feet
in front of a fourteen inch colour portable
and you call a stranger a liar

An opinion moulded
a belief is easy
the evidence ignored

Didn't you hear?

He was there
He saw his son
He watched
Fixed by fear and repulsion
as fists and teeth flew
Trapped and impotent in the chaos
A vulgar red fascination
oozed from a split lip

Then nothing
Over so quickly
That it seemed it could only be
a dream
Till
he reached down
to touch the warmth
of his son's slime and snot covered face
his birth remembered
now a bloody mess
in a nameless muddy field

STRIKE IV - one night

Like the rumbling treads of tanks
droning slowly surely nearer
Indistinct at a distance
            and in darkness
But turning menacing
            and clearer
Like hysterical children
clacking sticks on hollow logs
The batons beating
pounding perspex
a heartbeat sounding
sending fear

On and on the endless drumming
beating louder in its passing
drumming drumming drumming drumming
drumming
drumming
drumming
drumming

Two people hold against the darkness
but can't escape a fleeting shiver
a memory nagging stabbing
of a newsreel from a shipyard
Then the sound of their children crying
Lost in fear

STRIKE V - horse

The horse stands so tall
snorting
sneering
rolling eyes looking down with nervous arrogance
Its warm weight pressing into the crowd
The shining chestnut elegance
sweating and sinister
The smooth muscular beauty
still evident in the noise of panic
as the haltered beast
with the sweet smell of dung
teeth bared
crushes sideways
Stepping like a crazed tap-dancer
Bucking and nodding
Searching through blinkers
in moments of dumb fear

And on its back
almost unnoticed
sits a dark faceless figure
behind a mask of shame

Controlling

Time, like a slug, crawls past
Seconds
        extending
               with
                    repetition
Tense in the cold of early rising
Watching and waiting
Warm breath hanging in cold air
Watching and waiting
Anticipation
        numbed
               by
                    routine
Until, like an electric shock
An explosion of madness
As, at reckless speed, the wire windows
of different lives hurtle past
with their untouchable escort
Deflecting lung bursting verbal spears
Slung at one time colleagues
Who now
        turn
               knives
                    in backs
Treachery that cannot stand eye to eye
in a world of accusing mirrors
where knuckles whiten
Around
        thirty
               pieces
                    of silver

Decay

Whatever it was
you did it once
Whatever it was
you did it again
Whatever it was
you did it again
and again
and again
and again

Whatever you said
I heard it the first time
Whatever you said
you said it again
Whatever you said
you said it again
and again
and again
and again

Whatever you thought
did not really happen
Whatever you thought
you thought it again
Whatever you thought
you thought it again
and again
and again
and again

Whatever it was
you continue to do it
Whatever you said
has become repetition
Whatever you thought
has become the truth

Just desperation
just feeble words
inadequate expressions
hopeless words from the past

But then
when
our lips touched before they met
nothing said
clichéd thoughts
in a haze of sensuality
life itself
        in looks
        in staccato breaths
        in the heat of your body
        in such beauty
        and more...
...like the revealed meaning of the misunderstood
bearing witness at the court of truth
love like sunrise emerging
then still

like god smiling at the unbelieving

Selected paintings
from 2016 and 2017

Selected paintings
from 2016 and 2017

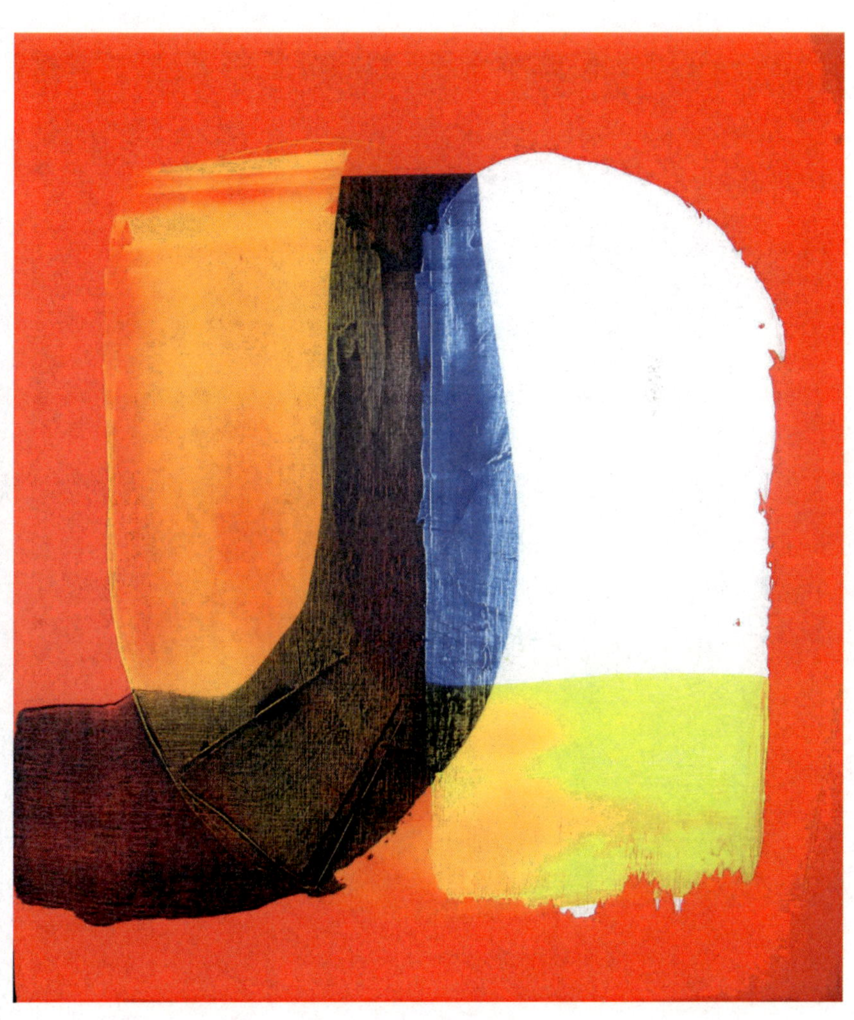

Overlap
Acrylics and inks on canvas 60 x 70cm

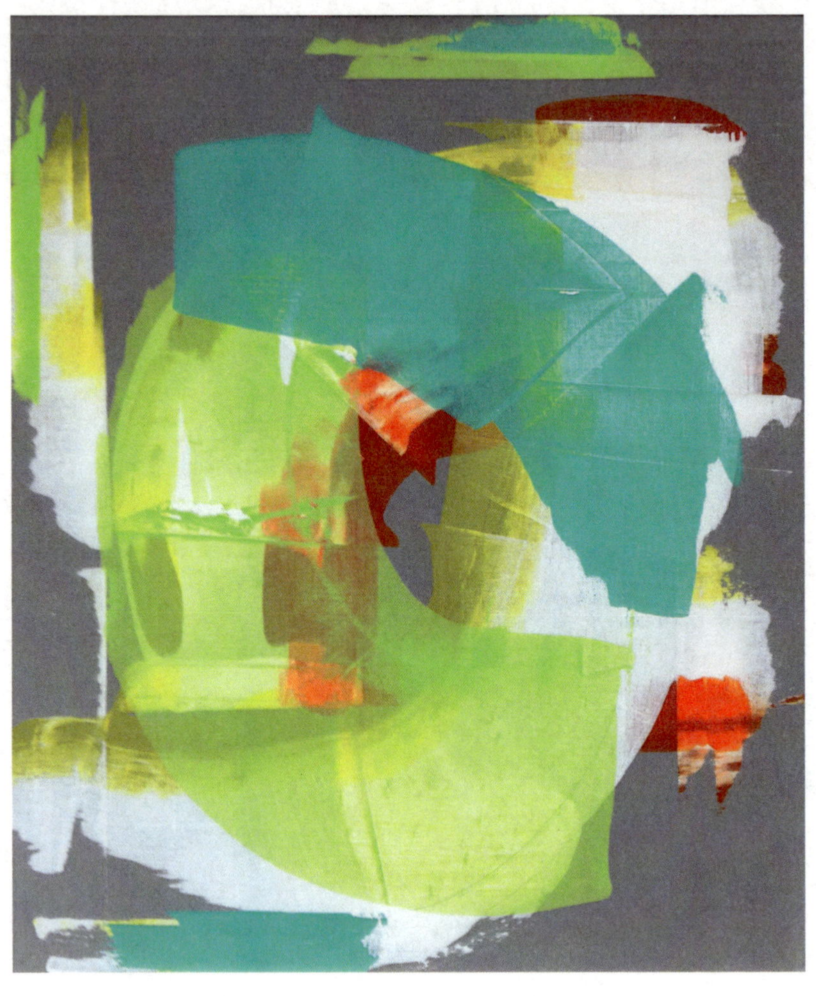

Rotation No1
Acrylics and inks on canvas 50 x 60cm

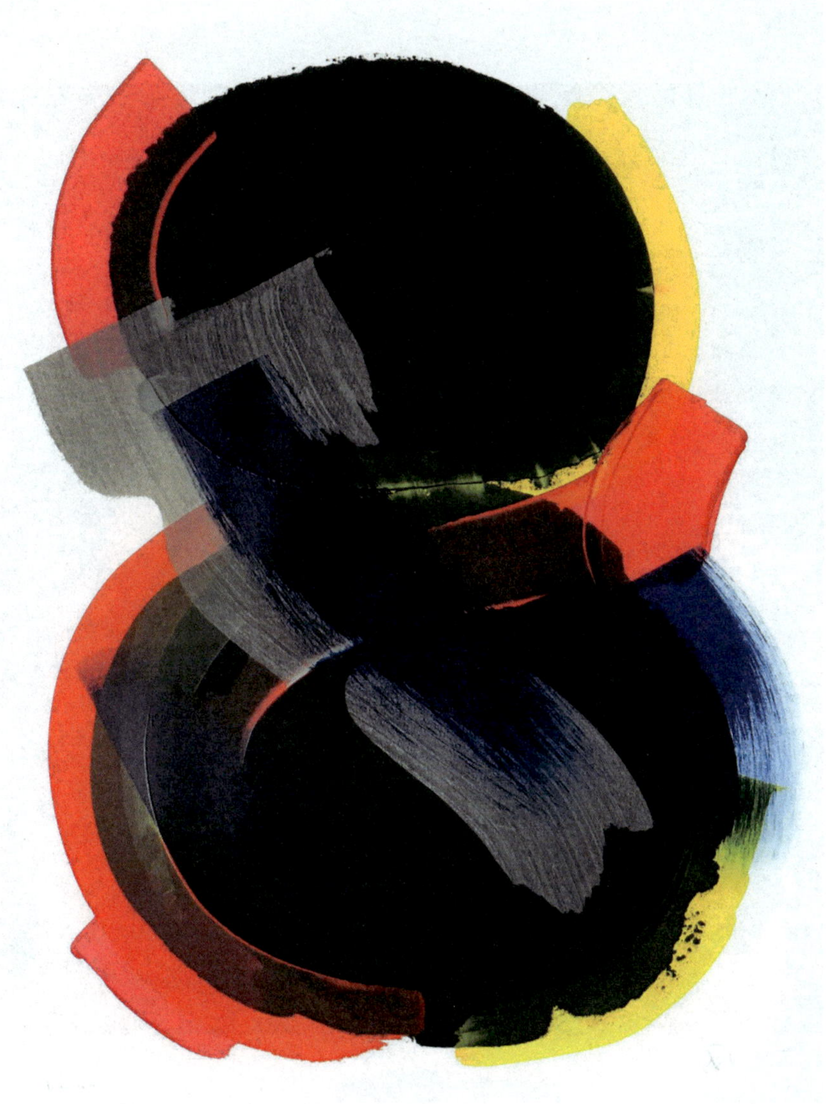

Balance
Acrylics and inks on paper 57 x 76cm

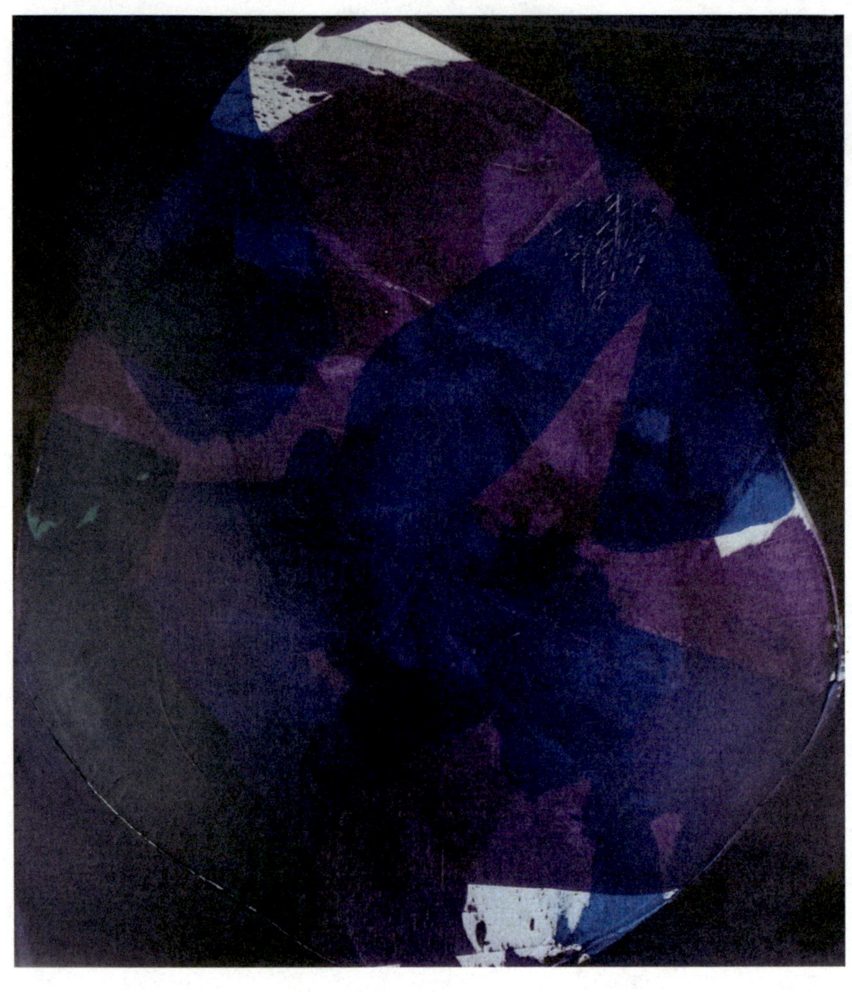

Stone No1
Acrylics and inks on canvas 60 x 70cm

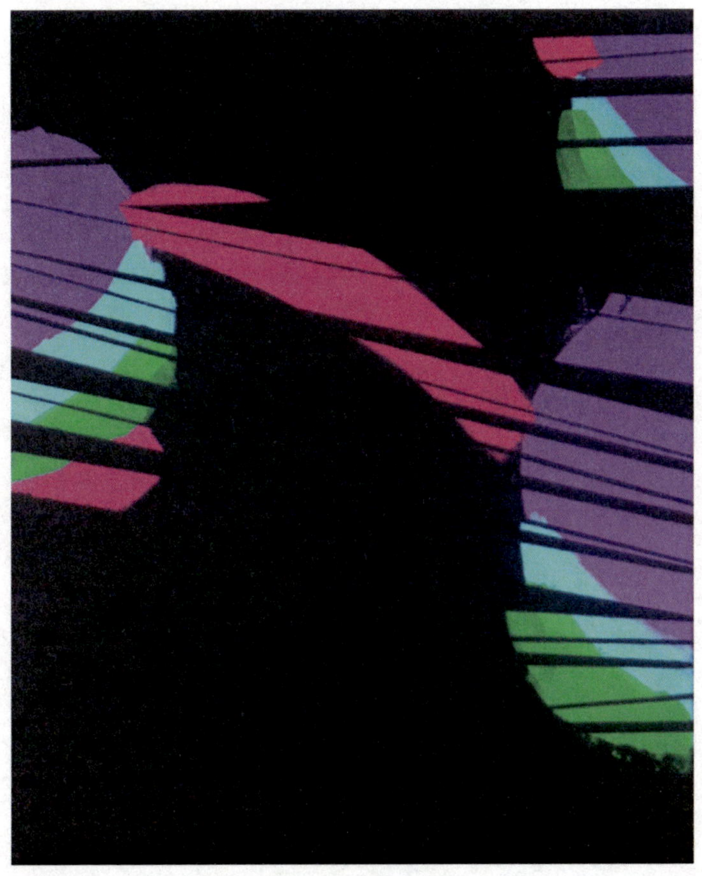

Untitled
Acrylics and inks on canvas 40 x 50cm

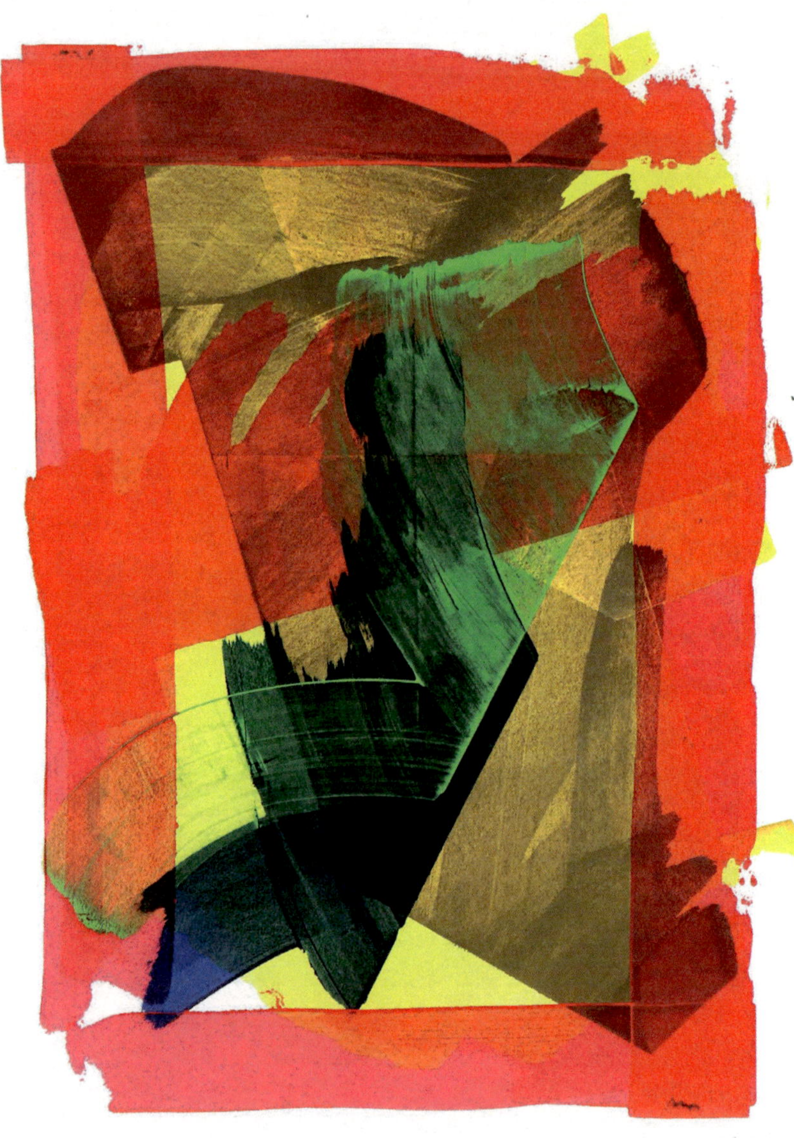

Framed
Acrylics and inks on paper 57 x 76cm

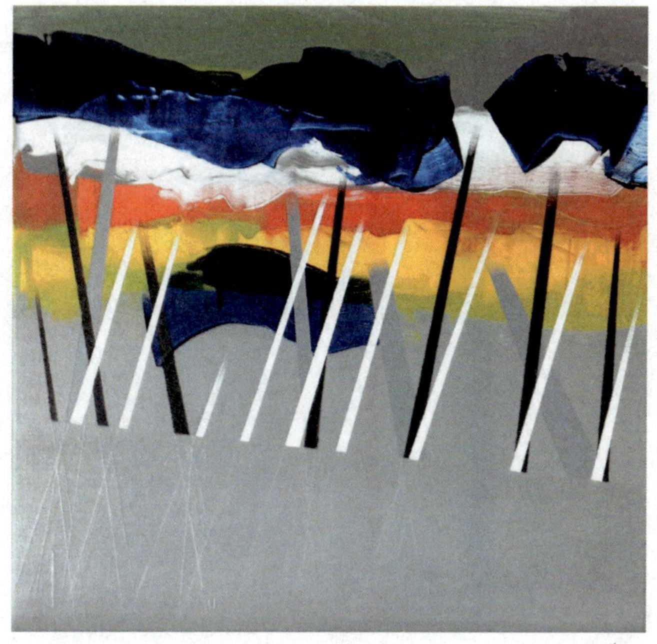

Not what it seems
Acrylics and inks on canvas 40 x 40 cm

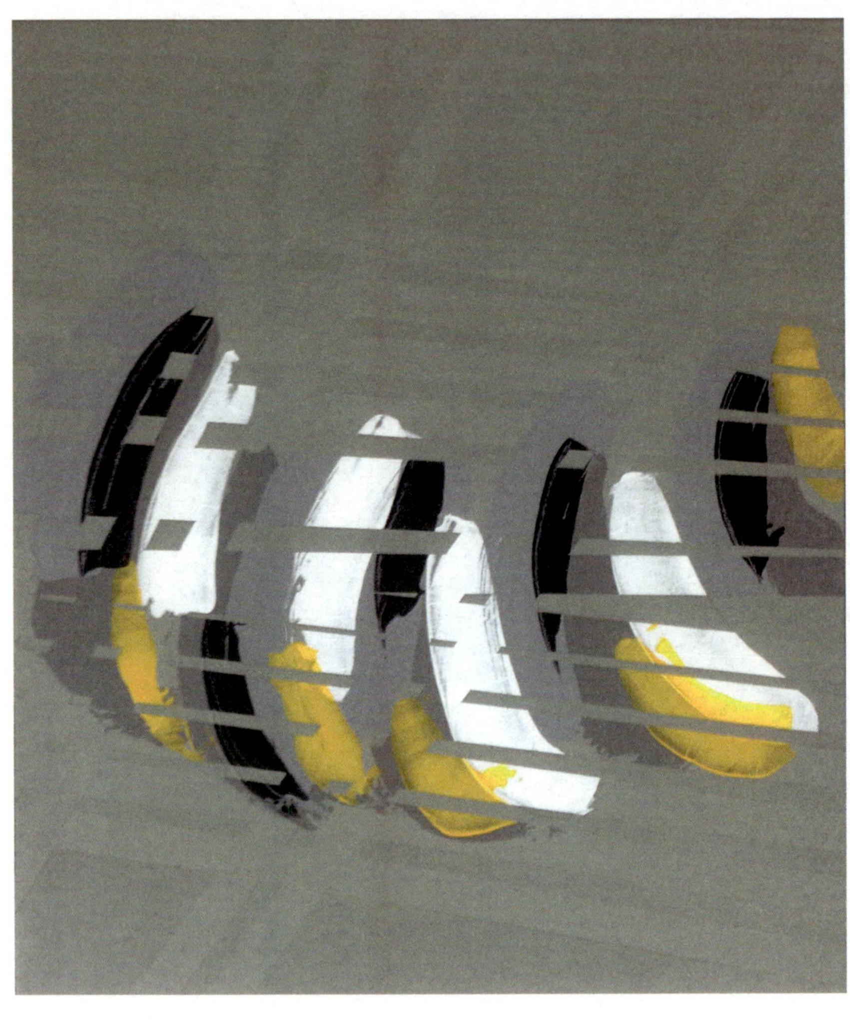

Untitled
Acrylics and inks on canvas 50 x 60cm

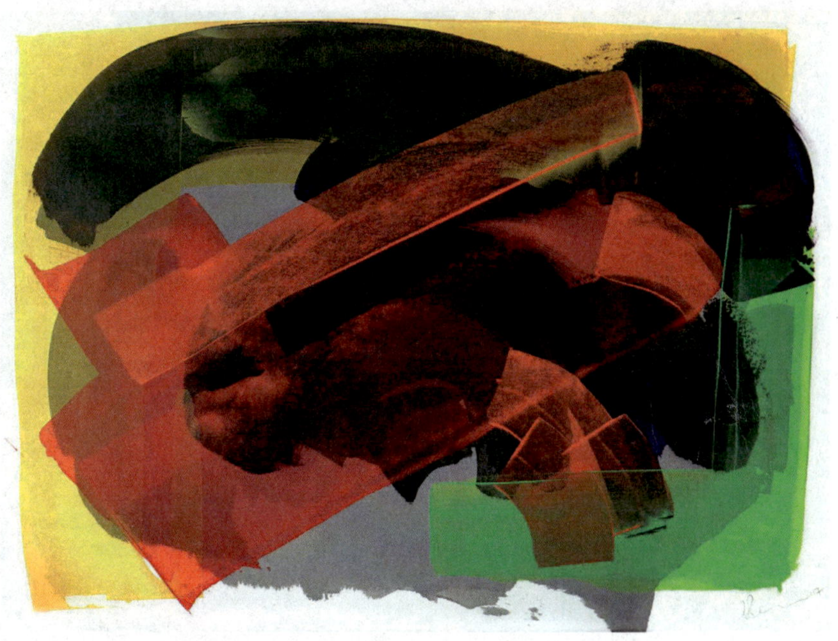

Untitled
Acrylics and inks on paper 76 x 57cm

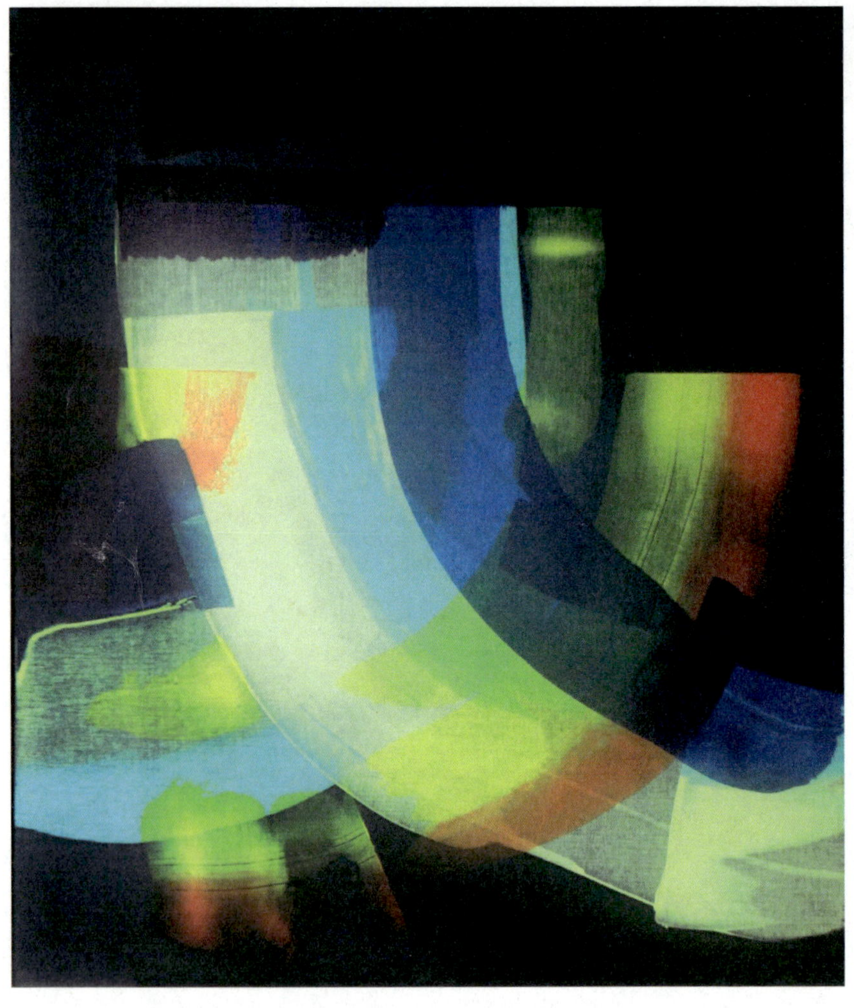

Field study No3
Acrylics and inks on canvas 60 x 70cm

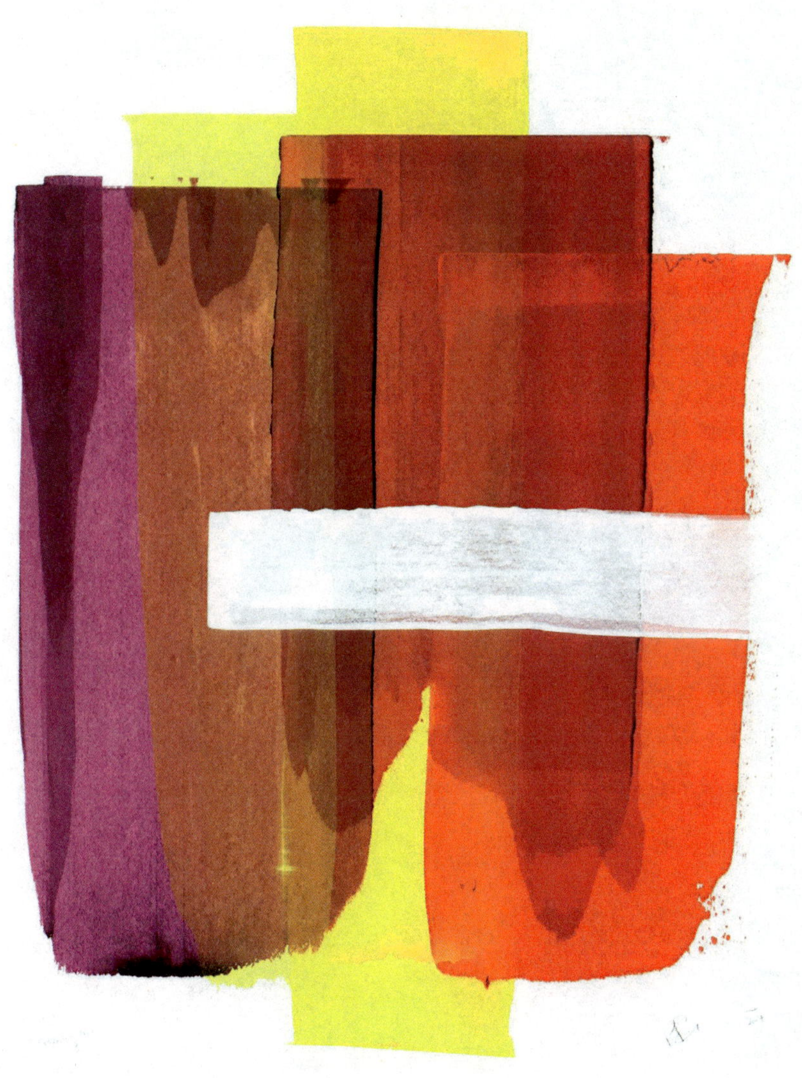

Crossing No1
Acrylics and inks on paper 57 x 76cm

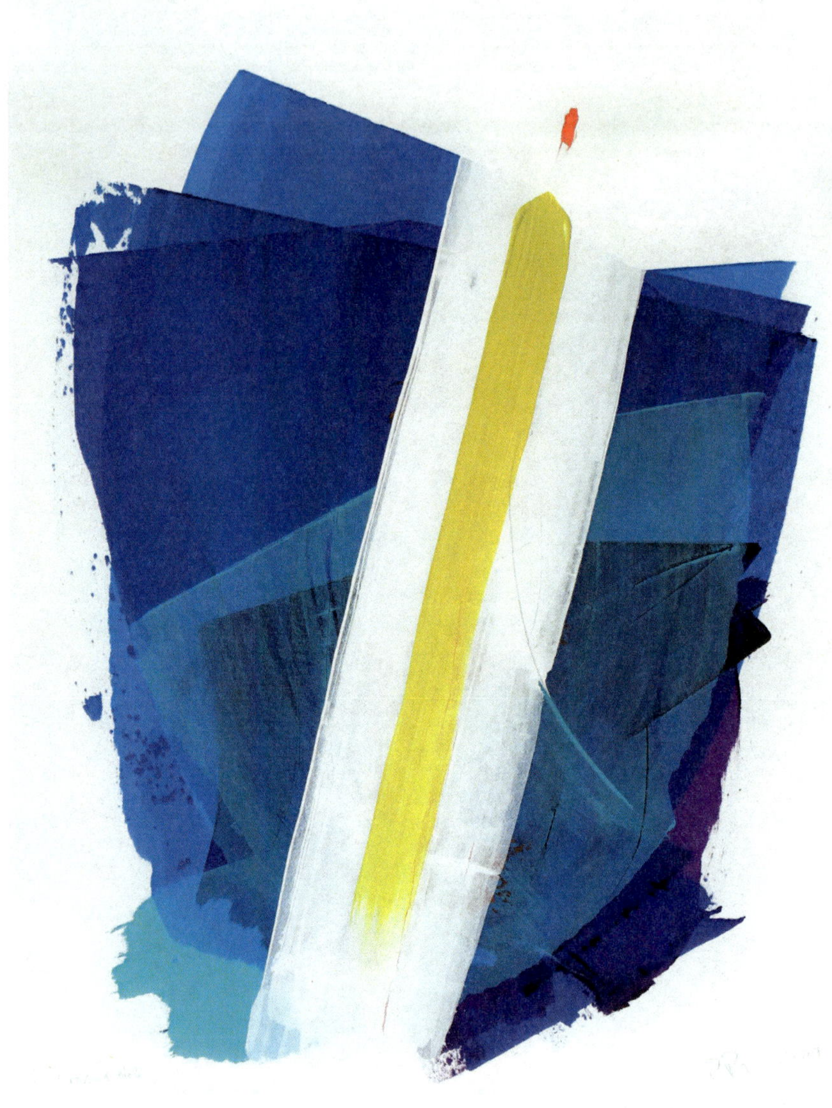

Crossing No2
Acrylics and inks on paper 57 x 76cm

A brilliant but silent façade
with sucking slot
with neon glow
calling coins from deep in pockets

insert

and punch in powder selection
click
the coin drops beyond recall
into a new life in a metal maze
whirr
click
click
hiss
water pissing into chemicals
in a plastic cup
hissing into compounds
with numbered prefixes
and / or suffixes
a final click
exhaustion and a return
to the same bright but silent façade
the same lame neon appeal
ignored
till the next insertion

Here is the news

Mr S.   of London
          of Middlesex
phoned the BBC
to ask for more light news
         more skate-boarding ducks
         more sun bathing, jacuzzi lounging rabbits
         more plastic bills for broken peckered toucans
all to make the world a brighter place
and to lift the gloom of everyday life

Just like Jane
who didn't want to see
the squalid houses at the end of the street
She drove past them
kept her eyes fixed on the road
and pretended no one lived there

In fact
no one saw the people who pretended to live there
except
the people who pretended to live next door
and the boys who pissed on the wall
pretending to be men
waving their little organs
in the drunken, spinning darkness

Dawn came cool and sleepless
Through tired eyes
vague and breathless

Lifting morning mists
revealed passing worlds
(so far from mine)
faded pastel shades
textures softened by the haze
shrouded villages
red roofed, still and shuttered
intruding on the landscape

Barges set solid in still water
looking to remain lifeless
Sinister forests seemingly dead
yet threatening to advance
and consume all
into their dark density

Oh for that heaving, driving machine to have stopped
or slowed at least
from its relentless passage
Oh to have kept sleep at bay
but there was no resisting
that firm caress

The ephemeral dream
for once was real
but beauty was, as ever
just passing

A child's view
(for my sister Pamela)

Pam's friend was the youngest sister of three
the naughty one
'I'm here, I'm here'
The middle sister was my age
the nasty one
or maybe middle sisters just don't like the anonymity
of their position
The eldest sister was sensibly old
and made up in wisdom for her lack of speed over the ground

Their house was dark green and gloomy
the rooms twice the size of ours
and their mum and dad were so big
that they seemed to be stooping under the ceiling

The younger sisters' dresses were flowered
tiny delicate flowers
The eldest sister had plain dresses
deep dark reds like curtain drapes
with white edging

And there was a smell
I don't remember exactly
but it wasn't unpleasant
It was just them

My sister said they were Catholics
and in my ignorance
I thought that must explain everything

In the same way that you cannot say 'I love you'
as a question
(even though you tried)
I cannot know what you know
when you say 'you know'
as a statement of fact

Things may be hot
When they're cool
And good when they're bad
And yet most of the awesome
Turns out to be average
You know what I mean?

Oh man
You should have seen it
It was like... just, wow!
Like, you know
(With or without a question mark)

Oh man
You should have tasted it
Like heaven
You know?
(heaven – noun)
An emotional construct
And I haven't been
And even if I had
I wouldn't be licking the floor
To see what it tasted like
Hoping to come back in a future life with the memory stored
You know?

Oh wow, just, you know
Not even a misplaced 'fantastic' or 'amazing'
Not a single verb or adverb in sight
You know?

A nod and an 'mmmmm'
Will have to do
Yeah?

DEAR Mr Burroughs

The old man's wordy lines
without pause
the typewriter's rickety click
The old prick dipper
notes
on an arse fuck fantasy
spurts
for once
on clean sheets

I'm walking down the street one day
Some kid says to me, 'HEY!
What are you looking at?'
And I say
What's it to you anyway?
Like it's act one, scene one, in a play
Happens every day

Meanwhile, on the internet
There are people who are so important in their own world
Telling me what they ate
Why they're late
What to wear and the best product for their hair
And there are people who care
Like it's act one, scene two in a play
Happens every day

And I'm walking down the street one day
To somewhere that isn't there
To a place that used to be
Over there was where
Was where
In black and white as clear as day
Like act one, scene three in a play
Or so they say

And on Sunday a country was invaded
It said so on the news
But now it's another day
And a little girl has been bitten by a dog
An actor divorced
The ongoing war is already in the past
The plot too hard to follow
Like it's act one, scene two in a play
But not today

Why go for fifteen minutes in the spotlight
When fifteen seconds will do

We're not laughing with you
We're laughing at you

And you will know my righteous anger

Not cold and calculating
And without the full fury with red mist
Almost casually

I committed murder
A moth after my cloth
Dispatched with the back of my hand
A life changing event
Especially for the moth

I consoled myself
That in a previous life
The moth had been
A bad tempered bull dog
A Conservative cockroach
Even a nasty butterfly
Or a banker

Now it's dead
To save my jumpers
Saved from becoming a bad moth
In my eyes

But even moths have to eat
And now I'm a killer
Maybe I'll come back as a battery hen
Or a lazy donkey
And get the beating I deserve

I am your travelling sales representative
I am your representative sales executive
I am your memory set to selective

I have a ripped memory of a road map
I have a satnav setting and a speed rap
I have a dream of life as an ex-pat

I am the hostess trolley of infatuation
I am the wallpaper of insinuation
I am the unfaithful interpretation

I have the automatic garage door of achievement
I have lived the hard life of investment
I have the human resources of resentment

I am the law loved and the land
I am the hope hung from the rope hand
I am the day dream of the bloody brand

I have the barbecue burns of bliss
I have never known the consuming kiss
I have only tasted the narcotic miss

I am the fondue set of another age
I am another stain on a torn out page
I am charity rattling tin of rage

I have the privilege of god's given right
I have the spray deodorant of sight
I have the soiled sheets of a sleepless night

I am the father of instinct and invention
I am the mother of pretention
I am the child of apprehension

I have the weight-loss wardrobe of spending
I have the alcoholic means of mending
I have the extra topping's unhappy ending

Don't make me do it

Fill my shoes with shit
Rub my eyes with grit
Just don't make me say I love you

Shock my nipples with wires
Pull my nails out with pliers
Just don't make me say I love you

Play on my darkest fears
Make me listen to Britney Spears
Just don't make me say I love you

Lock me in a cage of rabid rats
Let loose the fucking vampire bats
Just don't make me say I love you

Water-board me till I cry
Elevator music till I die
Just don't make me say I love you

Drop me in a sea of ice
Crush my fingers in a vice
Just don't make me say I love you

Break my bones with sticks and stones
Put maggots in my ice cream cones
Just don't make me say I love you

Then the terror turns into rubble
The words came tumbling at the double
Fumbling, mumbling, heart pounding
Astounding sounding simple words
I love you

And you said 'ditto'!

the usual Sunday afternoon stuff
bits and pieces
sorting this
tidying that
and looking through bits of paper
with odd notes scribbled
through the mist of drink
things written on beer mats
pages torn from diaries
scraps on the backs of bills

and in the middle of this meandering
a complete poem
several years old
and unusually long
(beyond the deadline that is the bottom of the page)

a love poem
bringing back kisses, longing and sadness
in equal measure
all there in touchable detail

the only thing I couldn't recall
was who the poem was about
and now I feel like shit
selfish

god bless america

ten-thirty saturday morning
nothing looks too hot in the rain
except peeling paint that shines
looking old and new at the same time

at least it would in a black and white
social documentary photograph

and there are three hookers
in micro-minis on a corner by the hudson
their square padded shoulders in leather
their white cone legs in stockings
with a good six inches
between the stocking tops and the skirt

their black umbrellas in frozen hands
their heels clicking

and this whole area is rust
with sprayed names on walls
to a height that looks out of reach

the few cars that pass
seem to be getting the hell out of here

and I wanted to see the guy who
got out of bed late
had a shit and a shave
drank half a pint of milk from the carton
checked the time
counted the dollars in his pocket
and thought
I know what I'll do today

with the temperature up
and the sun low
the long shadows of dizzy tall buildings
turn madison square park
into a sun-dial surface

and around mid-day
everyone was at least five minutes late for something
except
that is
those guys
sat on the benches around the park

they were bang on time
making a personal art
out of waiting
and for some reason
people don't look so convincingly hungry
when it's warm

and as I passed through
only just noticing
the difference between the walkers and the sitters
a guy in a purple sweat-shirt
and jeans and no socks
took his dick out
and without getting up
pissed a good fountain
right there in the park
causing people to walk wider
and a little quicker

there's not much else to say
about moments like that
it just seemed like a reasonable thing

for him to be doing

in new york

I saw this guy several times
always within a hundred yards
of the junction of 5th avenue and 42nd street

if he'd stood up straight
he'd have been a shit-kicking bare-knuckle fighter
or even
scrubbed up
some people's idea of an african prince

but instead
he had a blackboard
on a piece of string around his neck
and he wasn't promoting the best pastrami on rye in town

the board told his story
in neat white chalk
in small writing
which meant I had to get up close to read it

so, I'm stood close and reading
and he's unconcerned
and looking past and through me
and neither of us is in the least embarrassed

he'd fought in 'nam'
his wife left whilst he was away
taking his baby boy
and no one knew where they were
his mother had died within weeks of his return
he'd never known his father
he'd had insignificant jobs
but couldn't settle out of the army
now homeless and jobless and wifeless and childless

but he wasn't going to steal off anybody
and if some change could be spared
he'd be grateful

There must be something in that sense of outrage
that keeps their chins off the damn floor

They freed Nelson Mandela by buying the tee-shirts
and by not buying the oranges
and that got their peckers up
and made them feel a tiny bit black inside

But I can't help seeing these guys as compulsive wankers
in unclean sheets writing to the lonely hearts columns
but only after they've protested to the American ambassador
over yet another violation of basic good taste

Some days I drive too fast for the hell of it

Others get a buzz from power and its prospects
drink dripping from their chins
they don't see it as a game
but they sure play it as a game
and in the box ad it will say
"caring, sense of humour, wide range of interests"

But do they give flowers?
and what do they give at Christmas?
and how do they say "I love you"
without sounding ridiculous?
do they kiss differently?

They live in houses with no mirrors

Tricky moments

All that waiting
like a child in mid-December
Until, alone together at last

we watched TV
She lay on the settee
one leg over the arm
the other resting on the low back
and bit her nails
then sucked her fingers.

Was this body language?
Or just a comfortable position?

Like a scene from a cheap porn film
That you know you should laugh at
but which becomes erotic
for all its absurdity
and oh the embarrassment
of an erection now

All the words I wanted to say
seemed like drips from a tap
But, give myself fifteen minutes to say something

like
"would you like to make love?"
or
"would you like to go to bed?"
or just out with it
"Jesus H Christ, I want to fuck"

But in the end
fifteen minutes up
and a few more besides
I said nothing

Not for fear that she say "no"
but for fear that she might just say
PARDON!

I'd rather grow old than grow up
Growing up?
It just doesn't seem to happen

With her and her eyes of indeterminate age
(couldn't even make a guess to save my life)
and like all clichés it made me laugh
but I DID think I'd seen her somewhere before
not sure

So like a girl in a subtitled French film
where sexuality is discovered
through summer's open windows
where bodies are tanned and sheets are white

Afternoons forever on celluloid
without the taste of sweat
innocence and confusion atomised in the light beam
between projector and screen

But don't dare accuse me of wishing
I'm not one for filling empty spaces with dreams
not after smelling the cigarettes on her breath
it's just that
I would have fallen into her eyes
only
the subtitles kept changing
and I couldn't help watching her lips
for accidental synchronisation

The box

I thought of a line for a poem
            in which
I placed my thoughts inside a box
            a blue box
an exact cube

The sides
            2 metres wide
the walls
            one centimetre thick

There was no hole
            or lid
by which to enter the box
the thoughts filtered in
            by osmosis

I thought that this was
            very
            profound

And have you found the obvious question?
The question that I cannot answer

Why should the box be blue?

You threw the ball
said 'catch'
though with a hint of warning
and a slice of hope

but my hands were in my pockets

The ball fell to the floor
and we both just looked at it
disbelieving

The ball had been thrown softly
there was just enough distance and time
for me to remove my hands
from my pockets
and stand triumphant

I didn't

I let the ball hit me
refusing to play the game
seeing the test for what it was

a test

Offended at the idea
that a test was going to help
that I wasn't quick enough
that I didn't remember what I'd said

Lipstick

New traffic warden on the block
with lipstick overload
Fixed smile failing to convince
And all undermined by an ill-fitting uniform
baggy sleeves rolled up
trousers too long and hanging limp
in one-size-doesn't-fit-all style
over heavy boots

Badly fitting uniforms
were also worn by the spotty young boys
in a provincial French restaurant
Gastronomic class
Dried herbs scattered on everything
like one colour confetti
and even the blue jacketed boys
saw the funny side

The new traffic warden
seemed to see things differently
seemed to see herself differently
Her scarlet lip smile
a personal statement of defiance

The first real frost today
A white sky on the horizon fades to a soft clear blue overhead
There are still red and golden leaves falling
The air so sharp it's like pouring an iced liquid into my lungs
The sun so low and hidden by the trees
The glassy sparkling blanket of brittle grass
Hats and scarves against the prickly pinch

And those lost to fashion
look good and shiver

The speech

Tic toc
clock watching
as early evening falls on the cobbles
with the heel clicks
tic toc
time takes place somewhere else
the smell of soups lean on meat
makes for a smile of comfort
that brings out smiles on all the faces around
like sunlight on morning flowers

Smiling faces
not imaginary faces
but real faces
chinless
        blue eyed
                brown eyed
fair haired
        stub chinned
                an acceptable nose
out this night
        to come together
                as one
heading in the same direction
as the insane man
who steps over sleeping dogs
that only he can see

Around each corner
shambling with ill-defined purpose
they came
more
        and more
bonded by silence
        and anticipation
reassured by the smell of a leather jacket
drawn closer
by the nods and handshakes of strangers
unheard words in the ear

from someone recognised
          but never spoken to

A crowd embracing by numbers and anonymity...

Slowly aware of your own breathing
it's easier
          to let the body sway
to let the feet tap
to lean forward
          as if waiting to be kissed
aware of others' breathing
as the first clear words
like swirling snowflakes
melt on your face
make you imagine
          Bessie Smith
weaving spells of seduction around you
          and you alone
amongst who knows how many
right there
always set in rows on certainty
where the eye darts sideways
and your teeth clamp together
in embarrassment
          at the sight
of all the dropped jaws

The sound arcs
          in a half shout
the stage lit face
          is bleached out
tattered nerve ends twitch
at the swollen fingertips
of an outstretched hand
that holds you
          like cold love
then falls
          and flies

nettle stings the skin
as eyes too distant to focus
suck devotion out of open mouths

The warm air smothers
and wraps around the under-arms
that ache
lifted by hook bites
confuses
the speed of the footsteps
          with the heartbeat
with the deep breath
          and the white heat
that follows
          the whispered
                    lewd suggestions
that make you move your lips
muttered things
          that you had thought yourself
but never said

Casts out
          the Jezabel spirit
                    with the Jews
and fills the void of doubt
with the dripping intestines
ripped from sacrificial lambs
with a nervous laugh that says
ha ha
that's enough now
          it's gone too far...

...too late
  too late

At home
you wash the dirt from your hands
and wonder
what trickery
was this?

Dendrology
(the study of trees)

A mighty oak in the deepest wood
Tall and wide its branches stood
Sexy sap filled, the poet smitten
A poem waiting to be written
Its languid leaves tease the light
Glistening wet and colours bright
The autumn falling leaves a loss
Who gives a toss...?

Dad

Dad smoked from fourteen
Unfiltered
Useless
Never really tried to quit
Not even after a chest full of tubes
Bubbles in bottles under the bed
He didn't see the fear in my eyes
He didn't feel mum's anger
Useless

Uncle Jack
Mum's brother
Smoked from fourteen
Unfiltered
Never tried to quit
Just stopped on his sixty-fifth birthday
The inarguable example

Dad had plans and promises
Useless
But this was before we all had hopes
And unfulfilled aspirations
Before we all had to live our dreams
And consummate our potential
This was when you shut up
Sucked it up
And got on with it...

Dad had jokes and joy
Priceless

Dad had tricky football feet
Precious
And a Subbuteo flick
And time
Always time

When death came to our house
And we were broken

Mum let the pain show
The tears flow and wiped away mine
Lost her god and reason

Dad was quiet and uncertain
Useless
Dismissed
But he too was broken
Not knowing what he was meant to do

He went to work and paid the bills
Came home tired and kept it all inside
And as the jokes and stories returned over time
It was never quite right
Useless

Only the daily crossword kept them connected

But when I was low he let me win
Sunday night games
And at other times put me in my place

I stole
Mum, so disappointed
He told me off for getting caught
Two views to contend with

Years past

Then grandkids brought the light back
And even a little faith
Something to share

I'll never know the full story
Parents keep something back
But he wasn't useless
He was there
Every day

Maybe (cut up...)

Feet slightly apart and planted in concrete
Chest out, finger pointing certainty

I'm not so sure
I'd like to hear the alternatives
I'd like to see some options
I'm not so sure any more

And yet some people seem so absolutely bone-crushingly convinced
that they are right
Stating their opinions as facts
unable to contemplate opposition or other angles

Things look different from here
Things look grey not black and white
Grey in infinite shades and every shade spells intrigue

Self-belief in every footstep
in every breath
in every sideways glance
making those of us with doubts more doubtful than before

Faith feeds the demagogue

Made to feel guilty for not knowing the answers
I wish to remove the heart from my sleeve
and replace it with a question mark

Curiosity seems unchallengeable
Question follows question
No proof is required
and proof IS required
But facts only need to fail once
and they are nothing but old news

Is this the difference?
The inquisitive and the not?
Reflectors and absorbers?
Finishers and starters?

Doubters and fools
Maybe, maybe not...

You said that you loved me
but you said you loved ice cream
you said that you loved me
and you also loved to dream

You said that you loved me
but you said you loved to dance
you said that you loved me
and you loved to take a chance

You said that you loved me
but you said you loved new shoes
you said that you loved me
and you said you loved the blues

You said that you loved me
but you said you loved pink gin
you said that you loved me
and you loved a little sin

You said that you loved me
but you said you loved the cat
you said that you loved me
and that was simply that

You said that you loved me
but you said you loved the sea
you said that you loved me
and you wanted to be free

You said that you loved me
but you said you loved warm weather
you said that you loved me
but you didn't say forever...

Same song
(for Reg)

Some songs never leave
Years and memories gone
And you are the song that stays the same
The words sometimes a little vague
Mumbling
Stumbling through a line
And you are the song that stays the same
Every note
Every syncopated beat
Comes back
Not like it was yesterday
But now
The song that stays the same